Choosing a Mate

Choosing a Mate

by
Ken Stewart, D. Min.

Harrison House
Tulsa, Oklahoma

Unless otherwise indicated,
all Scripture quotations are taken from
the *King James Version* of the Bible.

4th Printing
Over 25,000 in Print

Choosing a Mate
ISBN 0-89274-341-7
Copyright © 1984 by Family Worship Center
P. O. Box 690240
Tulsa, Oklahoma 74169

Published by Harrison House, Inc.
P. O. Box 35035
Tulsa, Oklahoma 74153

Contents

1
Who Should
Have a Mate?

And the Lord God said, It is not good that the man should be alone; I will make him an help meet for him.

Genesis 2:18

Do you think that God created Eve because Adam was alone? Most people do. But that is not the case at all! If you will take a very close look at the above scripture, you will begin to see what I mean.

God plainly said, ''This man needs help!''

God created Eve to ''help'' Adam. The thing we have not understood is just what kind of help she was created to provide.

When we think of choosing a mate, it is usually the problem of being alone that we think we are going to resolve. But being alone is a problem that can only be resolved by having a personal, intimate, eternal relationship with God.

The purpose in having a mate is to provide the help we need in our relationship with God.

There are some people reading this who would have never gone through the hurt and the anguish they have experienced, if someone had only told them this truth from the Word of God.

Not everyone needs a mate to help them in their relationship with God.

Both Paul and Jesus made reference to this fact. Paul spoke of it in First Corinthians, chapter seven, as a ''gift.''

Jesus used very different terminology, as is recorded in the following words from Matthew's Gospel.

For there are some eunuchs, which were so born from their mother's womb: and there are some eunuchs, which were made eunuchs of men: and there be eunuchs, which have made themselves

**eunuchs for the kingdom of heaven's sake. He
that is able to receive it, let him receive it.**

Matthew 19:12

Let me speak to you in plain
language. He said, ''There are people
who have absolutely no sexual desire
because they were born that way. This
may be something physical, or it may be
mental. But one thing is certain—they
have no desire for any kind of sexual
involvement or relationship.'' That's the
first group.

Then He said, ''There's another
group that was made that way by men.
They are physically incapable of having
sex. And a third group make themselves
eunuchs for the sake of the Gospel.''

There is a clear distinction between
that third group and the first two. The
first two are incapable of a sexual relationship. Something physical makes
them incapable of that relationship.

But with the third group, it is not
something mental or physical. It is a
quality decision in an individual's heart

7

that he will put away all desire for any kind of sexual relationship. The ability to do that is referred to as a ''gift.''

To get a little more plain, if you have any sexual desire at all, or if any sexual desire can be aroused within you, then you ain't one of them eunuchs! You need a mate. You do not have that ''gift'' that Paul spoke about in First Corinthians, chapter seven. And, furthermore, you will need help in your relationship with God.

To state it as clearly as I know how, I will quote Paul in 1 Corinthians 7:2.

Nevertheless, to avoid fornication, let every man have his own wife, and let every woman have her own husband.

Every man and woman who cannot otherwise avoid fornication should have a mate—even those who have been married before.

Let's examine a little more carefully these statements I have been referring to of Paul's.

For I would that all men were even as I myself. But every man hath his proper gift of God, one after this manner, and another after that.

I say therefore to the unmarried and the widows, It is good for them if they abide even as I.

But if they cannot contain, let them marry: for it is better to marry than to burn.

1 Corinthians 7:7-9

In other words, some have this gift of God, and some don't. Everyone has his own gift. If Paul had that gift, thank God for Paul. But most folks don't.

Must I Stay Single If I'm Divorced?

I have already implied that the answer to the above question is "no." But there are a lot of people who are confused about this matter. They say, "I'm divorced, and I can't remarry." Who says?

If that's right, and if that's what the Bible teaches, then you ought to lose your sex drive when you get a divorce.

Let me repeat what Paul said:

9

Nevertheless, to avoid fornication, let *every* man have his own wife, and let *every* woman have her own husband.

1 Corinthians 7:2

That's another way of making the same statement made in Genesis 2:24. After God created man and woman, He said:

Therefore shall a man leave his father and his mother, and shall cleave unto his wife: and they shall be one flesh.

Genesis 2:24

Why Many are Single

The reason I have made these remarks is that most people have a desire for a mate. On the basis of information I have gleaned up to this moment, I can say that the reason many people choose to be single is certainly not because they desire to be without a mate.

There are thousands of single people who are afraid. They are afraid to get close to someone. They are afraid for someone to get close to them, because they have been hurt. They have been mistreated. Someone has taken advantage of them. They have been used. They are afraid.

Here's another reason a lot of people are single—guilt. I could elaborate on that, but I don't want to just dig at the problem. I have a solution.

For whatever reason you are single, there is a solution in the Word that will allow you to rise above that and have the mate God intends for you. And you don't want one until you get that one.

If God has a mate for you, there must be a way for you to figure out who that person is and how to get that relationship started.

Should Christians Date?

The world has played such games with this subject of dating that I'm going to go back to the beginning and act like you don't know anything about it. I'm going to act like you've never had a date.

The first thing God did after Adam became a living soul was to endeavor to

11

establish a relationship between himself and Adam. That's what Genesis 2:7-18 is all about—God doing everything He can to establish a personal, intimate, eternal relationship with Adam. He did this so that Adam would not be alone.

That's your number one priority: your personal, intimate, eternal relationship with God. But the second most important thing in your life is your personal, intimate, until-death-do-us-part relationship with a mate.

There's no point in you suppressing that. There's no point in you running from that. In fact, you can't outrun it. For that matter, friend, unless you're in one of those three classifications of eunuchs, you may run from it for the next fifty years, then wake up one day when you're 92 saying, ''Dear God, I wish I were married.''

Your first priority is your relationship with God. That means your second, third, fourth, and fifth priorities should all be affected by your first priority. That first priority shouldn't be affected by the others.

Don't ever allow your relationship with God to slip in order to have a mate. Keep your first priority first.

Your personal, intimate, until-death-do-us-part relationship with a mate will never be any better than your relationship with God.

Before you think about dating, you need to work on that personal, intimate, eternal relationship with God. When you are secure in that, you can have a successful personal, intimate, until-death-do-us-part relationship with another human being.

Wisdom From Genesis

Going back to the first chapter of Genesis notice this: God made things and saw that they were good. The chapter ends, **And God saw every thing that he had made, and, behold, it was very good** (Gen. 1:31). Now, when God says something is very good, it is very good. But He's the same God who said in Genesis 2:18, . . . **It is not good that the man should be alone . . . .** If He says something is not good, it is not good.

As a single, you may say, "You just told me the way that I'm living is not good." That's what God said. That doesn't mean, however, that you need to run out right now and do something about it.

Genesis 2:19,20 tells us:

And out of the ground the Lord God formed every beast of the field, and every fowl of the air; and brought them unto Adam to see what he would call them: and whatsoever Adam called every living creature, that was the name thereof.

And Adam gave names to all cattle, and to the fowl of the air, and to every beast of the field; but for Adam there was not found an help meet for him.

In other words, God said it's not good that man should be alone. But that didn't mean Adam ran out and grabbed the first monkey that came walking along. You

14

don't have to settle for the first person who comes your way, either.

Many times that's the problem—people get anxious. They say, "But God said it's not good that I'm alone. I've got to do something about this."

If God said it's not good that you should be alone, that was God's idea. Why don't you let Him do something about it?

Marriage Brings Favor

We've talked about what is not good. Now let's see what God said is good.

Whoso findeth a wife findeth a good thing, and obtaineth favour of the Lord.

Proverbs 18:22

I'm married, and I have the favor of the Lord. You may wonder, "You mean if you don't have a wife, you don't have the Lord's favor?" I didn't say that. But if you do have a wife, you do obtain the favor of the Lord. (That is, if you get the right wife.)

Setting Boundaries

We've established that the Word of God tells us, **. . . It is not good that the man should be alone** (Gen. 2:18). And, **Whoso findeth a wife findeth a good thing** (Prov. 18:22).

But here's one guideline the Word of God sets concerning this: **Thou shalt not covet thy neighbour's house, thou shalt not covet thy neighbour's wife, nor his manservant, nor his maidservant, nor his ox, nor his ass, nor any thing that is thy neighbour's** (Ex. 20:17).

Notice this: the Word of God does not say, ''Whoso findeth his neighbor's wife findeth a good thing.'' You say, ''I'm not stupid. Why are you pointing this out to me?''

Let me answer by telling about a man who called my office. He told my secretary, ''I phoned to get you to agree in prayer with me.'' She said, ''Well, sir, what did you want us to agree with you about?'' He said, ''I'm divorced. I have found this woman and I want to marry her.'' My secretary said, ''Well, that's fine.''

He said, ''Now, wait a minute. This is what I want you to agree with me on. She's married. I want you to agree with me that she'll get a divorce.''

The Word of God teaches, **Whoso findeth a wife findeth a good thing** (Prov. 18:22). But it's NOT talking about your neighbor's wife!

No Christian should ever desire or pursue another person's mate! That is a sin. Besides there are still plenty of good single people available!

You think you've got it hard! Look at old Adam. For a while all he had as possibilities were monkeys, turkeys, and pigs!

Be Equally Yoked

We find another guideline in Second Corinthians:

Be ye not unequally yoked together with unbelievers: for what fellowship hath righteousness with unrighteousness? (The answer is ''none.'') **and what communion hath light with darkness?** (None.)

And what concord hath Christ with Belial?
(None.) **or what part hath he that believeth with
an infidel?** (None.)

**And what agreement hath the temple of God
with idols?** (None.) **for ye are the temple of the
Living God; as God hath said, I will dwell in
them, and walk in them; and I will be their God,
and they shall be my people.**

2 Corinthians 6:14-16

Say this to yourself: "I am the temple
of the Living God. God dwells in me."

So many times we pray, "Oh, dear
God in heaven . . . ." God dwells in you.
Why don't you talk to the God on the
inside of you? You're the temple of God.

Say, "Spirit of God, rise up big on the
inside of me. Give me direction for this
day. Show me where I ought to go, and
who I ought to talk to. Tell me what you
want me to do, and I'll be obedient to
you. When I get off track a little bit, you
call my hand, and I'll get back on."

God is not way off somewhere. He
dwells in you. That's the reason you're
not to marry an unbeliever.

18

What should you do if you're dating an unbeliever? Break up!

"But, brother, I've been dating him a long time." Well, for a long time you've been wrong. "But I was dating him when I got saved." Break up with him. "But I want him to get saved." Break up with him.

"What will I say?" Say, "I'm saved. I can't go out with you anymore." If he says, "What does that mean?" tell him! Or, have you been waiting for someone else to witness to him?

"But I haven't been acting like I'm saved." Well, start acting like it. Start by telling him, "I'm saved."

"But he'll get the idea that I think I'm better than he is." You are! You are alive, and he is dead. To be alive is definitely better.

God told us not to be unequally yoked, and not to go after our neighbor's wife or husband.

Somewhere, among people who don't fall into those two categories, you can find a mate. God has one for you.

"I'm not ready yet!" That's fine. Put this information on the back burner. You'll need it one of these days. (You may need it sooner than you think.)

"No, I'll make up my own mind. When I get ready, then I'll be ready." Did you notice that Adam didn't wake up one day and say, "God, it's not good for me to be alone." It didn't happen that way. *God* said, "Adam, it's not good for you to be alone."

Listen to the Spirit of God

When the Holy Ghost talks, we ought to listen. A lot of people are talking today, saying many things. It doesn't make any difference whether you listen to some of them. But you need to listen to the Spirit of God.

Let's look for a moment at First Timothy 4:1-3:

Now the Spirit speaketh expressly, that in the latter times some shall depart from the faith, giving heed to seducing spirits, and doctrines of devils;

Speaking lies in hypocrisy; having their conscience seared with a hot iron; Forbidding to

marry, and commanding to abstain from meats, which God hath created to be received with thanksgiving of them which believe and know the truth.

This scripture is talking about now— the latter times. One translation says, ''giving heed to doctrines that demons teach.'' Did you know there are demons teaching today? Of course, they work through men and women.

''Forbidding to marry . . . .''

Have you gone through a divorce? Did you know that in these latter times most religious folks would forbid you to marry? And did you notice what that doctrine is called? That is a doctrine that demons teach.

Let's look at First Timothy 4:3 again:

Forbidding to marry, and commanding to abstain from meats, which God hath created to be received with thanksgiving of them which believe and know the truth.

You can eat anything edible if you believe and know the truth, and will receive the food with thanksgiving. We should approach marriage the same way.

Know the truth (don't approach it ignorantly), and go into it with thanksgiving in your heart.

One night I talked to a young lady at the front of the church. Tears were running down her face.

I asked, "What's the matter?"

She replied, "I'm getting married." I said, "Why are you acting like that?" She said, "Because I don't want to."

I said, "You don't want to what?" She answered, "I don't want to get married."

I said, "Now, wait a minute. You're getting married, and here you are crying about it, and telling me you don't want to." Her wedding was in two weeks.

I said, "Don't marry the man!" but she said, "I just have to." I said, "No, you don't."

"Yes, I do," she said. "I've got to marry him, because I told him I would."

I said, "Well, that's simple. Tell him you've changed your mind. Do you love him?"

"No," she replied. "But I'm going to marry him anyway."

I said, "You're making a mistake. This is foolishness. It's ignorance. Don't do it! Call him and break up. Tell him it's off—you're not going to do it."

She said, "I can't do that."

In case you're thinking she was pregnant (you shouldn't be, but maybe you are), she wasn't. She had, however, gotten involved immorally with this man. She thought because of that she had to marry him.

If you're involved in immorality with someone, you cannot enter into marriage with thanksgiving. Only a pure heart causes thanksgiving.

That girl should have asked God to forgive her for ever getting involved with that fellow. Instead, she went ahead with the wedding. Two years later, they got a divorce!

You Are Good

One of the reasons many divorced people never consider remarriage is because the devil told them they're not good.

I know that to be the truth. That's one of the things that happens in divorce, especially when a believer is put away by an unbeliever. I know what happens in the believer's mind.

For months, even years, they have an inner struggle over who they are. "I'm not what the Bible says," they feel. "I'm not the creature God said I am. I'm not the good person you tell me I am."

You ought to just stand up and yell, "Thank God I'm good!" The Bible says, **For every creature of God is good, and nothing to be refused, if it be received with thanksgiving** (1 Tim. 4:4).

Say this out loud: "I'm a creature of God. Therefore, I'm good!"

You're good! You're good. Did you know there are preachers who say to single people, "Don't marry somebody who has been married"?

Often they are really saying, "Those who have been married before are not

24

good.'' But the Word says every creature of God is good.

Don't expect rejection. Don't expect somebody to refuse you. People say, ''Oh, I wouldn't want to start talking to that person. I wouldn't want to go out with him. I've faced rejection so much.''

But the Bible says every creature of God is good. Quit expecting to be put down. Quit expecting to be used and mistreated. Expect to be received.

You're good! That's what the Scriptures say. You may ask, ''Isn't that particular passage talking only about pigs?'' That's what most people think when they read that. They think it's about the Jews not eating bacon.

But don't you know that if the Word can sanctify a pig, it surely will make you acceptable! You're a lot better than a pig, aren't you? If the Word will work on a filthy old pig, it'll surely clean you up so someone can receive you.

''But you don't know all the filth— the garbage—in my past.'' Well, it

certainly can't be worse than the life-style
of a pig!

2
What Do You Have to Offer?

Did you have a problem saying, "I'm good"? Most people do. So let's discuss that a little more.

Know therefore that the Lord thy God, he is God, the faithful God, which keepeth covenant and mercy with them that love him and keep his commandments to a thousand generations.

Deuteronomy 7:9

Do you know your Lord is God? If there were a thousand Buddhists with you in a meeting, you would have to say, "Old Buddha might have been a good man, but my God is God!" He said you have to know this.

Here's something else you need to know. Your God is the faithful God. The reason many people have problems in their Christian life is because they don't know God is faithful. They think He's capricious, double-minded, absent-minded, or playing games.

They use religious terms and tell you He's sovereign. But try telling them you believe, . . . **my God shall supply all your need according to his riches in glory by Christ Jesus** (Phil. 4:19). They'll accuse you of manipulating God. All you're doing is believing God is faithful.

Here's another thing you need to know. God . . . **keepeth covenant and mercy with them that love him and keep his commandments to a thousand generations** (Deut. 7:9).

The church I grew up in depended solely upon God's mercy. About the only scriptural prayer we knew was, ''God have mercy.''

We leaned heavily on God's mercy because we were ignorant of the Covenant. We didn't know anything about our Covenant rights. We didn't know who we were in Christ. We didn't know we were righteous. We didn't know we were the seed of Abraham.

We didn't know it was God's desire to bless us. We didn't know He wanted to prosper us. We didn't know He wanted to heal us—that He had already provided for all of that. But, thank God, we knew a little bit about his mercy.

When we would reach the end of our rope, we'd cry out, "God have mercy," and He would, because He's faithful. Now thousands of us have begun to learn about the Covenant. We're walking in the Covenant, living by the Covenant, speaking the Covenant, and confessing the Covenant. We're Covenant-minded, and we're expecting God to keep His Covenant.

Don't Forget God's Mercy

Some of us have gotten so Covenant-minded that we've forgotten God's mercy. We have actually said to people, "If you don't know what the Bible says and how to believe it and confess it, you can't expect to receive anything from God."

I beg your pardon. He's not forgotten His mercy. He's faithful in mercy, and He's faithful in Covenant. You'd better thank God that He is, because you don't always walk and live by the Covenant. That's when you need mercy.

What does this have to do with our subject? Keep reading, and you'll find out.

Notice, God . . . **keepeth mercy and covenant to a thousand generations** (Deut. 7:9). If a generation is 40 years, that's 40,000 years. That's long enough for you. Man has only been here about 6,000 years at the most. So we have at least 34,000 years of mercy and Covenant left. That ought to do.

I'm going to live until I'm satisfied with life. If that turns out to be 120 years, that's nothing compared to 34,000 years of Covenant and mercy.

Psalm 107:1 tells us:

O give thanks unto the Lord, for he is good: for his mercy endureth for ever.

Psalm 107:1

That's not a contradiction of Deuteronomy 7:9. If you live to be 120,

40,000 years seems like forever. The real truth of the matter is, His mercy does endure forever. The next verse, Psalm 107:2, says, **Let the redeemed of the Lord say so.**

Let me take a moment to tell you about a Bible training center graduate who was discussing these scriptures one day. He thought he had a great revelation from the Word of God.

This is what he was preaching. He said, ''When the devil comes to you and says, 'You're broke,' you should say, 'So?' Or, when the devil says, 'You're in pain—you've never hurt like this before,' you should say, 'So?,' because the Bible says, 'Let the redeemed of the Lord say *so*.' '' (Ps.107:2).

(There are better scriptures to use on the devil than that. First Peter 2:24 will do you a lot more good.)

The first part of Psalm 107:1 is what you're actually supposed to say: ''The Lord is good and His mercy endures forever.'' Do you know what the redeemed of the Lord have been saying instead? "The Lord killed my baby." "The Lord caused me to go bankrupt to teach me a lesson." "The Lord caused me to have an accident, be paralyzed from the waist down, and be strapped in this wheelchair so that He could teach me something."

This is what we are to say: "The Lord is good and His mercy endures forever."

The next two verses show us this passage is talking about us:

Let the redeemed of the Lord say so, whom he hath redeemed from the hand of the enemy;

And gathered them out of the lands, from the east, and from the west, from the north, and from the south.

Psalm 107:2,3

Have you been redeemed from the hand of the enemy? Are you from the East, West, North, or South? Then this must be talking about you.

Say this out loud: "The Lord is good and His mercy endures forever."

You need to know the Lord is good so you can believe you're good. That's

32

what this scripture has to do with our subject.

If you're having trouble believing you're good, then you don't have it firmly established in your heart that the Lord is good. If you're getting frustrated trying to see yourself as good, why don't you back off for a little while and work on seeing the Lord as good.

Get to Know Who God Is

In Genesis 1:26 God said, . . . **Let us make man in our image, after our likeness.** You're made to be like God.

Here is a basic principle you need to understand. Any time you have difficulty concerning the way in which you see yourself, there is a problem in your understanding of God.

You need to know Who the Father is, what the Father has, and what the Father can do. Then you'll know who you are, what you can have, and what you can do.

Your knowledge and understanding of who you are is tied directly to your knowledge and understanding of Who the Father is. You need to know the character of God.

An understanding that God is good, helps you come to grips with the fact that you are good. When you understand that God is faithful, you can be faithful.

People who are unfaithful in marriage relationships don't know the faithful God. I didn't say they weren't saved. But if they are unfaithful to their mate, they are lacking in their understanding of the faithful God.

When you understand Jehovah Jirah, (the One Who takes care of you from the day you're born until the day you leave this earth—and throughout eternity), you'll grow and develop. You'll not just be the person saying, "God, meet my needs." But you'll say, "God, show me someone who has a need I can meet."

Too many people feel they should be like the little woman who touched the hem of Jesus' garment. She said, **. . . If I may but touch his garment, I shall be whole** (Matt. 9:21).

God doesn't want you to be the one just touching the hem of His garment. He wants you to be the one with the garment on.

How are you ever going to do that? You have to know the Lord is good so you can see yourself as good. You have to see Him as Healer, so you can believe that when you lay hands on the sick they will recover.

You need to see Jesus as the Healer so much that you come to the point of believing if someone touches you, they're going to receive healing.

You must know who you are. So many times people start at the wrong point. They go to the Word to find out about themselves.

They've lived a life of sin and ungodliness and have never been taught anything except religious tradition. Somebody tells them, "The Bible has a lot of good things to say about you."

So they come to the Word thinking, "I'm going to find out about me." They read it, and it sends them into a spin. What they need to do, first of all, is find out about God. First John 4:17 says, **. . . as he is, so are we in this world.**

I've mentioned before that you need to find out Who the Father is, what the Father has, and what the Father can do. That will show you who *you* are, what *you* have, and what *you* can do.

When you have a good grasp of these six things, you will have a basic understanding of who the enemy is, what the enemy has, and what the enemy can do. That's nothing, nothing, and nothing!

Yet if you don't know who you are and Who the Father is, if you don't know what the Father has and what you have, if you don't know what the Father can do and what you can do—then the enemy is something. He can do something and he has something—your goods.

How are you going to turn that around? You have to know the Father, and you have to know yourself. A lot of people just stumble through life, hoping and praying things are going to turn out right.

They say, "One of these days, I'll meet a man and I'll fall in love. I'll get married and everything will be wonderful."

They have some silly idea of what it's going to be like. They have a romantic notion about someone riding up on a big white horse: "Oh, it's going to be something! He's going to treat me so nice. If I ever find the right person, then I'll get married and everything will be beautiful."

No, it won't—not unless you're the right person. It's more important for you to *be* the right person than it is to *find* the right person. We can't change the person you might meet one of these days. But we can do something about *you*! You may say, "You can't do anything about me. I'm not going to let you!"

Keep reading! This could change your life.

The Bible and Dating Today

We set the stage in the previous chapter to discuss dating. Yet, in the Word of God, there's absolutely no reference to the kind of dating that is done today. Some of you reading this, being serious students of the Word, have gone through the Bible looking for help on relationships. You might have found a certain story in the twenty-first chapter of the Book of Judges. It is something!

It is about the tribe of Benjamin. Because of a war, many of their men and women had been killed. The tribe was about to pass out of existence.

Somebody came up with a wonderful solution. They said, "In Shiloh there is a big dance about this time every year. All the young men should go there and hide in the bushes. When the girls start dancing, the men can sneak up and grab them and run off with them."

Isn't that wonderful? But I'll tell you what—it would be better than some of the things I've seen these days.

Seriously, most of the time when you read about relationships in the Bible, the parents found a mate for their children. Thank God we don't do that anymore.

I didn't want to marry the girl my mother picked out. I married another girl, Donna, a beautiful woman of God. I picked the right one!

You see, you're on your own. Yet, there are people who will try to help you. You know about those lovely people in the church. They'll say, ''Now, how old are you? You mean you're still single?''

Lots of people will try to help you. But in the final analysis, it's up to you.

What Is your Reason for Dating?

There are basically two reasons for dating: for fellowship, and to find a mate. Those are the only scriptural reasons I can find.

A lot of times people say they're dating for fellowship, when really they have a lot more than that in mind. They say, "I love fellowship," but they're playing games with you. Three dates and they're ready to get married.

Did you hear about the guy and gal who went on a date? The guy turns to the gal and says, "I . . . ." and she says, "I love you, too." He says, "I . . . ." She says, "I want to get married, too." What he was going to say was, "I think I ought to take you home."

You are going to have relationships with people. You can't live unto yourself. It's healthy and good for you to have relationships with those of the opposite sex. God intended that. It's healthy as far as fellowship is concerned. For those who desire marriage, it's healthy as far as finding a mate is concerned.

The first thing that has to be established in relationships is for you to decide why you're dating. Only you can make that decision.

Some people say, "I don't desire a mate; I don't have any interest in marriage." Yet invariably when they see a beautiful young woman (or handsome man) they start thinking, ''Maybe that's the one.''

I'm trying to get you to be honest with yourself. Many people are so dishonest with themselves that they end up being dishonest with everybody else. If you're going to be honest with other people, you have to be honest with yourself.

If you've ever gone out on a date, why did you go? You say, ''I've been sitting home for the last 15 years, brother!'' All right—you're dating for fellowship. ''No, I'm looking for a mate.'' Fine—I just want you to be honest with yourself.

Whether you desire a mate or fellowship, both are right. God just wants you to be honest with yourself. If you want a mate, admit it.

The next question that needs to be answered is this: ''Does the person you're dating have the same purpose you do?'' You probably have been in a situation where you had one thing in mind and the person you were dating had something else in mind. You were dating for fellowship, but they were thinking about marriage with a capital "M."

How do you avoid a situation like that? You ask questions. Communication is one of the most important things in any relationship. When somebody phones and asks you to go out, say, "Why do I want to go out with you?"

"They'd hang up!" Good. That would save you a lot of trouble. It might save you a lot of money and heartache, too!

"I wouldn't want to say something like that. I've been wanting to go out with her for six months. Now she's finally called and asked me for a date!"

Single Women and Dating

Women are doing that now. It's not scriptural, but they do it.

Let me tell you something if you're a single woman. You should never tell a man you love him until he's told you that first. Wait for him to say it first.

And after he's said it, don't you say it. Don't respond, "Well, I love you, too." Make him sweat awhile. Make him give himself for you.

Say something like this. "All right, you say you love me? Quit taking me out for hamburgers. Take me to the steak house. You love me? Show me some tangible evidence."

You may wonder, "What right do you have to teach like that? That's not scriptural." First John 4:19 says, **We love him, because he first loved us.** The scriptural pattern for marriage is that Jesus is the groom and we are the bride. And Jesus always takes the initiative in this relationship.

As a single woman, go ahead and take a fellow out and pay for everything if you want to—if that's what you want to do for the rest of your life. If you want to support him from now on, go ahead and start that way.

Communication Is Important

As I said, communication is important. If you can't discuss why you're dating, your relationship is not going to go anywhere. You've got to be able to sit down, look at one another, and say, "Why are we doing this? What do you want out of a date? Is this for the sake of fellowship, or are you looking for somebody to marry?"

You may say, "If I talked to the one I'm dating like that, he'd never come back." Good. If you keep messing around with that guy, one of these days you'll marry him and you'll be sitting in the den trying to talk to him. All he'll do is grunt and say, "I'm trying to read my paper—shut up!" You'll remember then that I told you to discuss why you were dating.

If you want to date for fellowship only, you ought to make that clear. There's nothing wrong with that.

It's all right to be single. "What scripture do you base that on?"

Jesus was single. Paul was single. That was all right with God. It's okay to be single. It's okay just to have fellowship.

The Bible tells us Jesus had fellowship with women. "Did He go out on a date?" At one point He seemed to be out with two women at the same time—Mary and Martha. One of them was listening to the Word and the other was cooking dinner. Jesus told them He would rather they both listen to the Word. "That wasn't a date." I didn't say it was, did I?

I just want to impress upon you that fellowship is okay. You don't have to wonder every time you go on a date, "Is this the person I'm going to marry?"

You may think I'm taking this subject of dating very seriously. I am. I've seen too many people hurt by a frivolous attitude.

Dating to Find Out Who You Are

You should never date for the purpose of finding out who you are.

Teenagers are taught to do that in our society. Parents tell them, "Son, the reason you ought to date a lot of different girls is so you can find out what kind of person you want to marry."

They are really saying that part of the purpose of dating is to find out who you are.

Then there are the people who get married and find that their mate pretended to be a totally different person while dating. They say, "That's not the guy I thought I married."

It's like the story about a man who met a woman with a beautiful voice. She sang like an angel. They got married. And when he woke up the next morning and saw her with her hair messed up and no makeup on, he quickly shook her awake. "Sing, woman, sing!" he begged her.

If you start dating people to find out who you are, you're only going to become more insecure. They'll tell you you're not who the Bible says you are.

They'll do things to convince you (if that's what you're going by) that you're not the person you thought you were.

You must go to the Word of God to find out who you are. Until you do that, you have no business going on a date.

A lot of people you date may not be as mature in the things of God as you are. They may not have the fruit of the Spirit in their life like you do. They may not turn out to be the sweet, nice, kind, wonderful person you thought they were. You may go home hurt and put down.

You'd better know who you are. Don't date to find that out. Don't date to reinforce who you think you are. And don't date for the purpose of ego.

Dating after Divorce

Divorce is one of the saddest things that happens in our society. It is a very destructive thing. Going through a divorce is similar to experiencing the death of a mate. Some people say it's worse.

I have met many Christians who are divorced from ungodly, selfish, stingy, mean unbelievers. Yet these dear, precious born-again people of God take all the blame for the divorce.

"It's all my fault," they say. Even though the person they married has been destroying them mentally and even physically for years, they are the ones who feel guilty.

As I mentioned, some have said that divorce is worse than the death of a mate. Let me tell you why. It's because you know that person who is still alive, could change. You know it could be different. You see other people get involved—you see the person you used to be married to dating somebody else.

In addition to that, some well-meaning individual comes along and says, "You need to start dating so you can find out who you are. Get out and mingle with people and re-establish in your own mind that you're really a wonderful, warm person."

Many books and magazines tell you that's the way to get your feet on the ground again. So, people follow that advice.

You talk about problems! Instead of finding out they are a warm, wonderful person, they get taken advantage of, used, abused, assaulted, and everything else. They wind up lower than before they had that date.

Get Established in the Word

Going out on a date won't establish you in who you are—but the Word of God will.

Some people who read this book should not date for the next ten years. They need that long to get hold of the Word and to let the Word get hold of them.

''Couldn't God do it overnight?'' Yes, God could do it overnight, providing you could take it overnight.

If you have been hurt, the thing that will help you the most is to get established in the Word.

Start talking about the healing. Start talking about the mending. Start speaking good things. Start looking in the Word and saying, ''Thank God I'm good. Thank God I'm righteous. Thank God I'm whole. Thank God I'm redeemed. Thank God I'm more than a conqueror. Thank God I'm a son of God. I'm a child of God. I'm blessed of God.''

You need to say that over and over again. You need to dwell on that. You need to renew your mind with that.

Let me ask you a question: Does the person you're dating know enough of the Word to help you move forward in your grasp of who you are? Or are they just going to tear down what you've done?

You may say, ''I don't know anyone who would reinforce me in the fact that I'm the righteousness of God, that I'm a joint-heir with Jesus, that I'm a wonderful person, and that I'm more than a conqueror.'' Then you should not be dating.

If dating is going to be a good experience for you, you have to know in advance who you are, where you've come from, and where you're going. You have to be determined always to please the Father—always to obey Him. Those things are important.

Find Out How Your Date Views You

Here's something else that will help you. Ask yourself questions like these:

"How does the person I'm dating (or the person I might go out with if I have the opportunity) view me? Do they see me as valuable and precious?"

Do *you* know you are valuable and precious? You have to know that, and it's important that the person you go out with knows that.

"How can I find out how they feel?" Tell them they're valuable and precious. If they look at you cross-eyed, you know you have the wrong one. If they say, "Valuable and precious—what do you mean by a statement like that?" you have the wrong one. There are so many things that need to be said while dating. I'm not going to go into all of them—there's simply not room.

But I do want you to understand this. You begin at the point of knowing who you are in Christ Jesus. Remember, your number one priority is your relationship with God. This relationship with God has an effect on your relationships with people.

Your personal relationship with another human being is never going to be any better than your personal relationship with God.

You must understand that a marriage, or even a personal relationship at the level of fellowship, is not just a spiritual relationship. It is a spirit, soul, and body relationship.

3
An Example for Pursuit

I see something happening in the Body of Christ among singles that disturbs me considerably. a lot of people are developing relationships that they want to be only spiritual.

That means they get together and study the Bible, pray, and discuss revelation knowledge from the Word. They discuss books and read to one another. They pray in tongues. It's a totally spiritual relationship.

You are a spirit, you have a soul, and you live in a body. You need to consider all three elements in a relationship.

What do I mean? Does the guy work? Does he take a bath? Does he know anything other than his great revelation? Is that T-shirt the only shirt he has?

Now don't get edgy because of what I just said—there are a lot of goofy people in this world. A relationship must be spirit, soul, *and* body. Since you are a combination of all three, you must consider all three.

You may be thinking, ''What difference does that make as long as he knows the Word of God?'' It makes a lot of difference.

Does her hair always look like that? (I didn't say good or bad.) Does she spend all her money on clothes? Can he cook if she can't? I'm trying to get you to be realistic.

It's all right to wear T-shirts and jeans—but not all the time. And no one prays and reads the Bible twenty-four hours a day. It simply is just not possible!

But if you marry this person, you will live with them twenty-four hours a day. Seriously consider what that may be like—how it would affect you spirit, soul, *and* body.

Seek a Mate Among Your Own People

If you're interested in finding a mate, go to your people. Who are your people?

The saved. The born-again. The righteous. The Spirit-filled. Get one who knows the Word like you know the Word.

"How can I find out if a person has these qualifications?" It's easy.

When you're talking on the phone to a person say, "Do you love Jesus?" "Oh, yes, I love Jesus." "Are you saved?" "Yes, I'm saved." "Are you filled with the Holy Spirit?" "I received the Holy Spirit when I got saved." Then pray in tongues. If they hang up on you, pray for them and go on! Get someone from among your own people.

Sent to Find a Wife

In Genesis 24:4, Abraham's servant is sent to find a wife for Isaac from among Abraham's people: **But thou shalt go unto my country, and to my kindred, and take a wife unto my son Isaac.**

Now listen to the servant's reply: **. . . Peradventure the woman will not be willing to follow me unto this land** (v. 5).

I can just see this. How many men have looked at a beautiful lady, and known in their heart she was the individual God had for them; and how many have said, "Lord, what if she won't follow me?"

You may ask, "Can you know in your heart who the right person is?" Absolutely. "You mean marriages are made in heaven?" I didn't say that. I said you can know in your heart who the right person is.

You know in your heart that you're born-again. That's your number one priority—your personal, intimate, eternal relationship with God. You have a guarantee that you can have a relationship with God because He made that your number one priority.

Unless you fall into one of those three classifications of eunuchs, you have a guarantee that there's a right person on this earth for you. God made that your second priority. That's your guarantee that there's somebody here for you.

Otherwise, God shouldn't have made that your second priority.

Don't go to God like the servant in Genesis 24: "God if she says 'no,' do you have somebody else?" How's that for believing God? (A real man of faith and power!)

And the servant said unto him, Peradventure the woman will not be willing to follow me unto this land: must I needs bring thy son again unto the land from whence thou camest?

And Abraham said unto him, Beware thou that thou bring not my son thither again.

The Lord God of heaven, which took me from my father's house, and from the land of my kindred, and which spake unto me, and that sware unto me, saying, Unto thy seed will I give this land; he shall send his angel before thee, and thou shalt take a wife unto my son from thence.

Genesis 24:5-7

God said He would send an angel before Him! I can hear it now, as you pray before you go to sleep tonight. "Angels, go forth, and get my mate."

And if the woman will not be willing to follow thee, then thou shalt be clear from this my oath: only bring not my son thither again.

And the servant put his hand under the thigh of Abraham his master, and sware to him concerning that matter.

And the servant took ten camels of the camels of his master, and departed; for all the goods of his master were in his hand: and he arose, and went to Mesopotamia, unto the city of Nahor.

And he made his camels to kneel down without the city by a well of water at the time of the evening, even the time that women go out to draw water.

And he said, O Lord God of my master Abraham, I pray thee, send me good speed this day, and shew kindness unto my master Abraham. Behold, I stand here by the well of water; and the daughters of the men of the city come out to draw water:

And let it come to pass, that the damsel to whom I shall say, Let down thy pitcher, I pray thee, that I may drink; and she shall say, Drink, and I will give thy camels drink also; let the same be she that thou hast appointed for thy servant Isaac; and thereby shall I know that thou hast shewed kindness unto my master.

Genesis 24:8-14

No, you don't need to buy ten camels in order to find yourself a wife! But look carefully at these scriptures.

In verses 1 through 9, Abraham's servant swears before God to find a wife for Isaac. In verse 10, he goes to Mesopotamia. When he gets there, he goes to the well. The women are coming out to draw water. This was the custom. The servant arrived to look for a wife for Isaac when all the women of the city had come out to draw water!

So with all those women there, the servant prayed. His prayer appears to be about the nuttiest prayer in the Bible. He said this: ''God, I'm standing here by the well. I'm going to say to one of these women, 'Give me a drink.' Let her answer, 'Not only will I give you a drink, but I'll draw water for all your camels.' If she says those words, I'll know she is the one.''

Isn't that a fine way to find a mate? It's like you going to the water fountain at your church and praying, ''Father, when a woman walks up here, I'll say, 'Give me a drink.' I'll know she is the one, because she'll answer, 'Not only will I give you a drink, but I'll fill the radiator in your car full of water.' '' That's how it sounds!

And it came to pass, before he had done speaking, that, behold, Rebekah came out, who was born to Bethuel, son of Milcah, the wife of Nahor, Abraham's brother, with her pitcher upon her shoulder.

And the damsel was very fair to look upon, a virgin, neither had any man known her: and she went down to the well, and filled her pitcher, and came up.

Genesis 24:15,16

I told you a relationship must involve spirit, soul, and body. This lady was very attractive.

And the servant ran to meet her and said, ''Let me, I pray thee, drink a little water of thy pitcher.

And she said, Drink, my lord: and she hasted, and let down her pitcher upon her hand, and gave him drink.

And when she had done giving him drink, she said, I will draw water for thy camels also, until they have done drinking.

And she hasted, and emptied her pitcher into the trough, and ran again unto the well to draw water, and drew for all his camels.

And the man wondering at her held his peace, to wit whether the Lord had made his journey prosperous or not.

Genesis 24:17-21

He's a real man of faith. Here it's happening, just like he said, and he's wondering, "Is this the one?"

I have had people tell me, "I prayed, and God brought someone into my life who is wonderful. They have all the qualities I prayed about. They're the kind of person I asked God for. We love each other. We're both born-again and filled with the Spirit of God. We're both growing in the Word and love God with all our hearts. How can I be sure they're the right one?"

They never will be sure—not if they keep thinking like that. They received what they prayed for. But they didn't believe it when they prayed, so they're "wondering."

This servant's prayer was being answered, and he was "wondering."

Do you know what wonder is? It's camouflaged doubt—a fancy kind of doubt—that's all. The servant didn't expect the answer to his prayer to come to pass. He was wondering, ''What's happening? She's watering all my camels. Isn't that amazing?''

There are several things I want to point out to you. As far as Rebekah knew, this man was a nobody. This was not Isaac—this was a servant. Rebekah was not trying to impress this man. He didn't come there with gold hanging all over him. He hadn't shown her any shiny jewels yet. He just had ten dirty old camels. He'd been traveling for hours to get there.

Why did Abraham send his servant instead of going there himself? Because Abraham was well-known. Had he gone, somebody would have tried to impress him.

Look out when people start trying to impress you. Don't you try to impress them. Did you know that is the basis of most dating? A guy is trying to impress a gal, and a gal is trying to impress a guy.

That's what it's all about. That's usually the way the game is played.

But Rebekah was not trying to impress this servant. Her true character was shining through by the way she treated him. The problem in most relationships is that you don't see the true character of the person until you're so deeply involved that it hurts to get out.

What is so sad about that is that many of these people go ahead and marry anyway. They think that will hurt less than getting out of the relationship. It always hurts more.

Why do they do it then? Usually they have the false notion that they can change the person after they marry them.

If you can't change them before you marry them, you certainly can't change them afterwards.

See Others as Valuable and Precious

There are some excellent principles involved in this story. We've talked about the importance of how your date views you. Rebekah treated this servant in such a way that he knew she viewed others as valuable and precious. a person like that makes a good friend, as far as Jesus is concerned.

Greater love hath no man than this, that a man lay down his life for his friends. Ye are my friends, if ye do whatsoever I command you.

Henceforth I call you not servants; for the servant knoweth not what his lord doeth: but I have called you friends; for all things that I have heard of my Father I have made known unto you.

John 15:13-15

Watch people and notice whether they see others as valuable and precious. If they do, you know they will make a good friend.

Jesus commanded us to love one another or to see one another as valuable and precious. When He sees you doing that, He says, ''There's my friend.''

That's what Abraham's servant was doing. His prayer was not so silly after all. Hear what was behind it. He was saying, "If I can find a woman who will treat me like I'm valuable and precious, I know when she meets Isaac she will treat him the same way."

I want to push that a little bit further. Watch how your date treats other people, and you can figure out how he'll treat you when he's no longer trying to make an impression.

If you're associating with someone who treats you like royalty, but treats everybody else like dirt—look out. Your turn to be walked-on is coming. One of these days they'll stop trying to impress you, and they'll treat you like they treat everyone else.

There's a strong principle involved here. That's exactly what Jesus does. He watches how you treat other people before He says, "There's my friend."

Going to church and singing about friendship with Jesus doesn't make you His friend. Seeing others as valuable and precious does.

When you find someone who sees others that way, you know he'll be the same way with you. That type of person is kind, loving, gentle, caring, and helpful.

Then you may find someone who's rough, mean, cruel and doesn't have the time of day for people. He shrugs them off and ignores them. He won't talk to them and says horrible things about them. Watch out. He'll treat you the same way.

"Oh, no, he loves me." No, he doesn't. If he treats others that way, he doesn't know what love is.

Look for a Giver

Notice something else about Rebekah. She was a giver. She wasn't trying to impress the servant—but to water ten thirsty camels she had to be a giver.

Real love is constant giving. Givers make good lovers. You don't want somebody who's stingy.

My advice to single women is, before you marry a man look him right in the eye and say, "Do you have the money to support me? Can you finance me? Do you know Who your Source is?"

"He'd never come back." Good. He's one tightwad you won't have to deal with.

Rebekah was a giver. She was a person who saw others as valuable and precious. She was one of Isaac's own people. That's three of the major ingredients of a lasting relationship.

Don't Hunt a Mate

There's something else I would like to share with you. Rebekah was just doing her job, minding her own business when this servant came along. She was not out hunting a man.

You say, "I would be in bad shape if I weren't looking for a man. I've been looking for four years and haven't found one yet. What would happen if I quit looking?" Maybe he'd find you.

Let's go back to Genesis, chapter 2. I would like to point out to you that

Adam was not looking for a mate. He was minding his own business, doing what God told him to do.

God said, "Adam, I want you to name all the creatures I've made." Adam started naming them. Whatever he called them, that would be their name forever.

But notice, Adam wasn't looking for a mate. God said, "I'll make a creature that's appropriate for you. I'll take care of that."

Adam just went on, minding his own business. There he was naming all the monkeys, and he was about to become the father of the whole human race.

There are a lot of people who get uptight about finding a mate. They think, "I have to be looking for somebody. I have to be expecting the right person to come along."

To those who think, "I've got to go looking for a mate. I've got to get involved," remember: Adam didn't. Isaac didn't. Rebekah didn't. They just went on doing their jobs.

Rebekah was about to become the bride of the wealthiest bachelor on the face of the earth. You know what she was doing? She was watering dirty camels.

You may say, ''If I get involved in developing my relationship with God, and forget about trying to find a mate, I'll never get married.''

I beg your pardon! If God can bring a rich bachelor into the life of a young girl as she's watering camels, He can bring your mate along. You just concentrate on developing your relationship with God.

Make Your Own Decision

There's one other thing I want to show you from Genesis 24.

And they called Rebekah, and said unto her, Wilt thou go with this man? And she said, I will go.

Genesis 24:58

So many people get the idea, ''When God shows me my mate, I'm going to hear a voice from heaven. God is going to tell me, 'This is the one!' God will make up my mind for me.''

Notice Rebekah said, "I will go." You have to make your own decision. You have that right, that privilege, that responsibility. No one else can live your life for you.

The servant couldn't make up Rebekah's mind for her. It finally came time for her decision. Did you notice she had never had met Isaac? She didn't have a picture of him. The servant didn't bring an 11- by 14-inch photo over to her and say, "Ain't he sweet?"

I want you to know this happened by the Spirit of God. Rid your mind of the world's foolish notions about how to find a mate, and get your relationship with God like it ought to be.

Take care of your number one priority. Get acquainted with God—who He is, what He has, and what He can do. Get acquainted with who you are, what you have, and what you can do. Get comfortable with who you are in Christ Jesus.

Believe that just as God intends for you to have a relationship with Him, He also intends for you to have a relationship with another human being if you want it. But you must decide, "I will."

Don't think that you're just going to fall into it. Don't expect to hear bells and see lightning. Don't expect that butterflies will come flittering by and that the moon will turn to gold. Get all that silly stuff out of your head.

Don't Be Anxious

I want to leave this thought with you as I conclude. Philippians 4:6 tells us, **In nothing be anxious . . .** (*American Standard Version*).* I want you to say this out loud: "I will be anxious for nothing." Friend, that includes a mate.

Too many singles are anxious in this area. I've shared many things to slow you down, to get you to quit being anxious, and to get you to stop and take

*(Nashville: Copyright © 1901 by Thomas Nelson & Sons. Copyright © 1929 by International Council of Religious Education.)

a good inventory of the things in your life.

I don't want you to make another mistake if you've already made one. If you have never been married, and have never made a mistake in a relationship in terms of getting married and divorced, I'm trying to keep you from ever making that mistake.

I believe I am sent from God for your benefit to keep you from going through the tragic experience of divorce, or of dating someone and having it turn into a horrible situation.

Remember: you are good, and God wants everything in your life to be good. He wants you to have that mate who is just right for you!

As Pastor of Family Worship Center in Tulsa, Oklahoma, Dr. Ken Stewart is very conscious of Satan's efforts to destroy marriages and lives. His extensive knowledge of God's Word is always presented in profound, yet practical, truths which have helped many to have meaningful lives and successful family relationships.

Dr. Stewart attended Brite Divinity School, Texas Christian University, where he received his Master of Divinity degree and his Doctor of Ministry degree.

He is the author of several books and teaching tape series and is in much demand as a speaker, traveling throughout this country and abroad ministering God's Word.

For a complete list of tapes and books by Dr. Stewart, write:

Family Worship Center
P. O. Box 690240
Tulsa, OK 74169

Feel free to include your prayer requests and comments when you write.